SWEET DREAMS

THIS JOURNAL BELONGS TO

DATE: /   /   TIME: /   /

MY THOUGHTS BEFORE SLEEP

WHAT HAPPENED?

MY EMOTIONS

PEOPLE IN MY DREAM

SKETCH

MY INTERPRETATION / FINAL THOUGHTS

DATE: /   /   TIME: /   /

MY THOUGHTS BEFORE SLEEP

WHAT HAPPENED?

MY EMOTIONS

PEOPLE IN MY DREAM

SKETCH

MY INTERPRETATION / FINAL THOUGHTS

DATE: / /   TIME: / /

MY THOUGHTS BEFORE SLEEP

WHAT HAPPENED?

MY EMOTIONS

PEOPLE IN MY DREAM

SKETCH

MY INTERPRETATION / FINAL THOUGHTS

DATE: /   /   TIME: /   /

MY THOUGHTS BEFORE SLEEP

WHAT HAPPENED?

MY EMOTIONS

PEOPLE IN MY DREAM

SKETCH

MY INTERPRETATION / FINAL THOUGHTS

DATE: /   /   TIME: /   /

MY THOUGHTS BEFORE SLEEP

WHAT HAPPENED?

MY EMOTIONS

PEOPLE IN MY DREAM

SKETCH

MY INTERPRETATION / FINAL THOUGHTS

MY THOUGHTS BEFORE SLEEP

WHAT HAPPENED?

MY EMOTIONS

PEOPLE IN MY DREAM

SKETCH

MY INTERPRETATION / FINAL THOUGHTS

DATE: /   /   TIME: /   /

MY THOUGHTS BEFORE SLEEP

WHAT HAPPENED?

MY EMOTIONS

PEOPLE IN MY DREAM

SKETCH

MY INTERPRETATION / FINAL THOUGHTS

DATE: /   /   TIME: /   /

MY THOUGHTS BEFORE SLEEP

WHAT HAPPENED?

MY EMOTIONS

PEOPLE IN MY DREAM

SKETCH

MY INTERPRETATION / FINAL THOUGHTS

DATE: /   /   TIME: /   /

MY THOUGHTS BEFORE SLEEP

WHAT HAPPENED?

MY EMOTIONS

PEOPLE IN MY DREAM

SKETCH

MY INTERPRETATION / FINAL THOUGHTS

DATE: / /   TIME: / /

MY THOUGHTS BEFORE SLEEP

WHAT HAPPENED?

MY EMOTIONS

PEOPLE IN MY DREAM

SKETCH

MY INTERPRETATION / FINAL THOUGHTS

DATE: /   /   TIME: /   /

MY THOUGHTS BEFORE SLEEP

WHAT HAPPENED?

MY EMOTIONS

PEOPLE IN MY DREAM

SKETCH

MY INTERPRETATION / FINAL THOUGHTS

DATE: /   /   TIME: /   /

MY THOUGHTS BEFORE SLEEP

WHAT HAPPENED?

MY EMOTIONS

PEOPLE IN MY DREAM

SKETCH

MY INTERPRETATION / FINAL THOUGHTS

DATE: /   /   TIME: /   /

MY THOUGHTS BEFORE SLEEP

WHAT HAPPENED?

MY EMOTIONS

PEOPLE IN MY DREAM

SKETCH

MY INTERPRETATION / FINAL THOUGHTS

DATE: /   /   TIME: /   /

MY THOUGHTS BEFORE SLEEP

WHAT HAPPENED?

MY EMOTIONS

PEOPLE IN MY DREAM

MY INTERPRETATION / FINAL THOUGHTS

DATE: /   /   TIME: /   /

MY THOUGHTS BEFORE SLEEP

WHAT HAPPENED?

MY EMOTIONS

PEOPLE IN MY DREAM

SKETCH

MY INTERPRETATION / FINAL THOUGHTS

DATE: /   /   TIME: /   /

MY THOUGHTS BEFORE SLEEP

WHAT HAPPENED?

MY EMOTIONS

PEOPLE IN MY DREAM

SKETCH

MY INTERPRETATION / FINAL THOUGHTS

DATE: / /   TIME: / /

MY THOUGHTS BEFORE SLEEP

WHAT HAPPENED?

MY EMOTIONS

PEOPLE IN MY DREAM

SKETCH

MY INTERPRETATION / FINAL THOUGHTS

DATE: /   /   TIME: /   /

MY THOUGHTS BEFORE SLEEP

WHAT HAPPENED?

MY EMOTIONS

PEOPLE IN MY DREAM

SKETCH

MY INTERPRETATION / FINAL THOUGHTS

DATE: /   /   TIME: /   /

MY THOUGHTS BEFORE SLEEP

WHAT HAPPENED?

MY EMOTIONS

PEOPLE IN MY DREAM

SKETCH

MY INTERPRETATION / FINAL THOUGHTS

DATE: / /   **TIME:** / /

MY THOUGHTS BEFORE SLEEP

WHAT HAPPENED?

MY EMOTIONS

PEOPLE IN MY DREAM

SKETCH

MY INTERPRETATION / FINAL THOUGHTS

DATE: /   /   TIME: /   /

MY THOUGHTS BEFORE SLEEP

WHAT HAPPENED?

MY EMOTIONS

PEOPLE IN MY DREAM

SKETCH

MY INTERPRETATION / FINAL THOUGHTS

DATE: /   /   TIME: /   /

MY THOUGHTS BEFORE SLEEP

WHAT HAPPENED?

MY EMOTIONS

PEOPLE IN MY DREAM

SKETCH

MY INTERPRETATION / FINAL THOUGHTS

DATE: / / TIME: / /

MY THOUGHTS BEFORE SLEEP

WHAT HAPPENED?

MY EMOTIONS

PEOPLE IN MY DREAM

SKETCH

MY INTERPRETATION / FINAL THOUGHTS

DATE: / /   TIME: / /

MY THOUGHTS BEFORE SLEEP

WHAT HAPPENED?

MY EMOTIONS

PEOPLE IN MY DREAM

SKETCH

MY INTERPRETATION / FINAL THOUGHTS

DATE: / /   TIME: / /

MY THOUGHTS BEFORE SLEEP

WHAT HAPPENED?

MY EMOTIONS

PEOPLE IN MY DREAM

SKETCH

MY INTERPRETATION / FINAL THOUGHTS

DATE: / /   TIME: / /

MY THOUGHTS BEFORE SLEEP

WHAT HAPPENED?

MY EMOTIONS

PEOPLE IN MY DREAM

SKETCH

MY INTERPRETATION / FINAL THOUGHTS

DATE: /   /   TIME: /   /

MY THOUGHTS BEFORE SLEEP

WHAT HAPPENED?

MY EMOTIONS

PEOPLE IN MY DREAM

SKETCH

MY INTERPRETATION / FINAL THOUGHTS

DATE: /   /   TIME: /   /

MY THOUGHTS BEFORE SLEEP

WHAT HAPPENED?

MY EMOTIONS

PEOPLE IN MY DREAM

SKETCH

MY INTERPRETATION / FINAL THOUGHTS

DATE: /   /   TIME: /   /

MY THOUGHTS BEFORE SLEEP

WHAT HAPPENED?

MY EMOTIONS

PEOPLE IN MY DREAM

SKETCH

MY INTERPRETATION / FINAL THOUGHTS

DATE: / /   TIME: / /

MY THOUGHTS BEFORE SLEEP

WHAT HAPPENED?

MY EMOTIONS

PEOPLE IN MY DREAM

SKETCH

MY INTERPRETATION / FINAL THOUGHTS

DATE: / /   TIME: / /

MY THOUGHTS BEFORE SLEEP

WHAT HAPPENED?

MY EMOTIONS

PEOPLE IN MY DREAM

SKETCH

MY INTERPRETATION / FINAL THOUGHTS

DATE: /   /   TIME: /   /

MY THOUGHTS BEFORE SLEEP

WHAT HAPPENED?

MY EMOTIONS

PEOPLE IN MY DREAM

SKETCH

MY INTERPRETATION / FINAL THOUGHTS

DATE: /   /   TIME: /   /

MY THOUGHTS BEFORE SLEEP

WHAT HAPPENED?

MY EMOTIONS

PEOPLE IN MY DREAM

SKETCH

MY INTERPRETATION / FINAL THOUGHTS

DATE: /   /   TIME: /   /

MY THOUGHTS BEFORE SLEEP

WHAT HAPPENED?

MY EMOTIONS

PEOPLE IN MY DREAM

SKETCH

MY INTERPRETATION / FINAL THOUGHTS

DATE: /   /   TIME: /   /

MY THOUGHTS BEFORE SLEEP

WHAT HAPPENED?

MY EMOTIONS

PEOPLE IN MY DREAM

SKETCH

MY INTERPRETATION / FINAL THOUGHTS

DATE: / /   TIME: /   /

MY THOUGHTS BEFORE SLEEP

WHAT HAPPENED?

MY EMOTIONS

PEOPLE IN MY DREAM

SKETCH

MY INTERPRETATION / FINAL THOUGHTS

DATE: /   /   TIME: /   /

MY THOUGHTS BEFORE SLEEP

WHAT HAPPENED?

MY EMOTIONS

PEOPLE IN MY DREAM

SKETCH

MY INTERPRETATION / FINAL THOUGHTS

DATE: /   /   **TIME:**   /   /

MY THOUGHTS BEFORE SLEEP

WHAT HAPPENED?

MY EMOTIONS

PEOPLE IN MY DREAM

SKETCH

MY INTERPRETATION / FINAL THOUGHTS

DATE: /   /   TIME: /   /

MY THOUGHTS BEFORE SLEEP

WHAT HAPPENED?

MY EMOTIONS

PEOPLE IN MY DREAM

SKETCH

MY INTERPRETATION / FINAL THOUGHTS

DATE: /   /   TIME: /   /

MY THOUGHTS BEFORE SLEEP

WHAT HAPPENED?

MY EMOTIONS

PEOPLE IN MY DREAM

SKETCH

MY INTERPRETATION / FINAL THOUGHTS

DATE: / /   TIME: / /

MY THOUGHTS BEFORE SLEEP

WHAT HAPPENED?

MY EMOTIONS

PEOPLE IN MY DREAM

SKETCH

MY INTERPRETATION / FINAL THOUGHTS

DATE: /   /   TIME: /   /

MY THOUGHTS BEFORE SLEEP

WHAT HAPPENED?

MY EMOTIONS

PEOPLE IN MY DREAM

SKETCH

MY INTERPRETATION / FINAL THOUGHTS

DATE: /   /   TIME: /   /

MY THOUGHTS BEFORE SLEEP

WHAT HAPPENED?

MY EMOTIONS

PEOPLE IN MY DREAM

SKETCH

MY INTERPRETATION / FINAL THOUGHTS

DATE: / /   TIME: / /

MY THOUGHTS BEFORE SLEEP

WHAT HAPPENED?

MY EMOTIONS

PEOPLE IN MY DREAM

SKETCH

MY INTERPRETATION / FINAL THOUGHTS

DATE: / /   TIME: / /

MY THOUGHTS BEFORE SLEEP

WHAT HAPPENED?

MY EMOTIONS

PEOPLE IN MY DREAM

SKETCH

MY INTERPRETATION / FINAL THOUGHTS

DATE: / /   TIME: / /

MY THOUGHTS BEFORE SLEEP

WHAT HAPPENED?

MY EMOTIONS

PEOPLE IN MY DREAM

SKETCH

MY INTERPRETATION / FINAL THOUGHTS

DATE: /   /   TIME: /   /

MY THOUGHTS BEFORE SLEEP

WHAT HAPPENED?

MY EMOTIONS

PEOPLE IN MY DREAM

SKETCH

MY INTERPRETATION / FINAL THOUGHTS

DATE: /   /   TIME: /   /

MY THOUGHTS BEFORE SLEEP

WHAT HAPPENED?

MY EMOTIONS

PEOPLE IN MY DREAM

SKETCH

MY INTERPRETATION / FINAL THOUGHTS

DATE: /   /   TIME: /   /

MY THOUGHTS BEFORE SLEEP

WHAT HAPPENED?

MY EMOTIONS

PEOPLE IN MY DREAM

SKETCH

MY INTERPRETATION / FINAL THOUGHTS

DATE: /   /   **TIME:**   /   /

MY THOUGHTS BEFORE SLEEP

WHAT HAPPENED?

MY EMOTIONS

PEOPLE IN MY DREAM

SKETCH

MY INTERPRETATION / FINAL THOUGHTS

DATE: / /   TIME: / /

MY THOUGHTS BEFORE SLEEP

WHAT HAPPENED?

MY EMOTIONS

PEOPLE IN MY DREAM

SKETCH

MY INTERPRETATION / FINAL THOUGHTS

DATE: /   /   TIME: /   /

MY THOUGHTS BEFORE SLEEP

WHAT HAPPENED?

MY EMOTIONS

PEOPLE IN MY DREAM

SKETCH

MY INTERPRETATION / FINAL THOUGHTS

DATE: /   /   TIME: /   /

MY THOUGHTS BEFORE SLEEP

WHAT HAPPENED?

MY EMOTIONS

PEOPLE IN MY DREAM

SKETCH

MY INTERPRETATION / FINAL THOUGHTS

DATE: /   /   TIME: /   /

MY THOUGHTS BEFORE SLEEP

WHAT HAPPENED?

MY EMOTIONS

PEOPLE IN MY DREAM

SKETCH

MY INTERPRETATION / FINAL THOUGHTS

DATE: / /   TIME: / /

MY THOUGHTS BEFORE SLEEP

WHAT HAPPENED?

MY EMOTIONS

PEOPLE IN MY DREAM

SKETCH

MY INTERPRETATION / FINAL THOUGHTS

DATE: / /   TIME: / /

MY THOUGHTS BEFORE SLEEP

WHAT HAPPENED?

MY EMOTIONS

PEOPLE IN MY DREAM

SKETCH

MY INTERPRETATION / FINAL THOUGHTS

DATE: / /   TIME: / /

MY THOUGHTS BEFORE SLEEP

WHAT HAPPENED?

MY EMOTIONS

PEOPLE IN MY DREAM

MY INTERPRETATION / FINAL THOUGHTS

DATE: /   /   TIME: /   /

MY THOUGHTS BEFORE SLEEP

WHAT HAPPENED?

MY EMOTIONS

PEOPLE IN MY DREAM

SKETCH

MY INTERPRETATION / FINAL THOUGHTS

DATE: /   /   TIME: /   /

MY THOUGHTS BEFORE SLEEP

WHAT HAPPENED?

MY EMOTIONS

PEOPLE IN MY DREAM

SKETCH

MY INTERPRETATION / FINAL THOUGHTS

DATE: /   /   TIME: /   /

MY THOUGHTS BEFORE SLEEP

WHAT HAPPENED?

MY EMOTIONS

PEOPLE IN MY DREAM

SKETCH

MY INTERPRETATION / FINAL THOUGHTS